Racism

Aladdin Books Ltd 2008

Designed and produced by
Aladdin Books Ltd

First published in 2008
in the United States by
Stargazer Books
c/o The Creative Company
123 South Broad Street
Mankato, Minnesota 56002

Illustrator: Christopher O'Neill

The author, Jen Green, has written extensively for young people
on social issues and other topics.

Printed in the United States

Library of Congress Cataloging-in-Publication Data

Green, Jen.
  Racism / by Jen Green.
       p. cm. -- (Thoughts and feelings)
  Includes index.
  ISBN 978-1-59604-153-0 (alk. paper)
  1. Racism--Juvenile literature. I. Title.

HT1521.G696 2007
305.8--dc22
                    2007009189

Racism

Jen Green

Stargazer Books

Contents

Introduction

These children are in the same year at school. They come from different cultures, but they all get on well together. But a few people treat those from other cultures badly. This is racism. The children in this book will share with you some ideas on how to deal with racism.

Racists miss out on many friendships.

Racism can be really hurtful.

Say "NO!" to racism.

What Is Racism?

Last week the class discussed racism. Marcus said that racism is treating someone unfairly because of his or her culture—this means having a different religion or a different way of doing things. Grace said racism is also picking on someone because he or she comes from a different country or has a different skin color.

Racism can happen anywhere.

Racism is being mean because a person's skin is a different color.

If someone is rude about a person's culture, he or she is racist.

▶ Name-calling

There are different ways in which people may be racist. It is racist to call a person a rude name or to bully someone, just because he or she comes from a different culture or a different country.

Why is he always calling me names?

Out of my way you *#?ø-**!

◀ Why Can't I Play?

Racism can be ignoring a person or leaving him or her out of a game, just because of the color of a person's skin, or his or her culture. Racists try to make others feel as if they don't belong.

▶ Judging Others!

Deciding what you think about a person before you get to know him or her properly is called prejudice. Racist people decide not to like someone just because of his or her skin color, religion, or culture, or even because of his or her clothes—without even knowing the person!

Story: Being Prejudiced

1 The class was asked to bring food to share, for a picnic in the park.

2 Kim and Jane thought they knew all about the kind of food that Anu ate.

3 In fact, Anu brought pizza. Next time, she brought curry —they all loved it!

Kim and Jane were unfair to Anu.

Kim and Jane were prejudiced. They had fixed ideas about Anu, because of her culture. Racist people are prejudiced. They choose to dislike someone who is different, without getting to know him or her. Kim and Jane felt they were better than Anu because her culture was different from theirs. This is racist. All cultures are equally special.

▶ It's Not Funny

Some racists make fun of the way other people talk, and then say they are just teasing. But it's not teasing if someone ends up feeling hurt or left out. Racism is not funny.

◀ Fixed Ideas

It is racist to have fixed ideas about people who come from the same culture, even if those ideas seem good. Each person is different. Everybody deserves to be treated as if he or she is special.

▶ It's Hurtful

When you get upset, you may use hurtful words rather than telling the person why you are angry with them. Name-calling is unfair. It hurts people and it doesn't solve anything. It's much better to tell the person what they have done to make you angry.

What do you know about racism, Jon?

"I'm Jewish. Last year there was a gang of bullies at school. One day they cornered me and asked me for money. When I said no, they started saying all Jews were stingy. A teacher heard them and stopped it. The bullies were prejudiced about Jewish people and had fixed ideas about me, without even knowing me."

The History Of Racism

Columbus said he discovered America in 1492.

But Native Americans lived there a long time before then.

Columbus said it was a new continent...

...not to the people already living there!

Paul and Ade are reading a history book. The history of racism goes back a long way. For instance, hundreds of years ago, Europeans traveled to lands where people already lived. They claimed the lands as their own and were unfair to the people who lived there. Racism has affected many people in many different countries.

▶ Good Times

Sam's grandparents were born in Germany. But when they were young, they had to leave because a very racist group, called the Nazis, began to attack Jews. Six million Jews were killed by the Nazis, just because they were Jewish. Sam is very proud to be Jewish.

◀ Native Peoples

Nascha is Navajo, one of the first peoples of North America. Around 150 years ago, European settlers in America forced the Navajo off their land and treated them very badly. Nascha enjoys living in the United States, but she is also very proud of her Navajo culture. Her name means "owl."

▶ Two Cultures

Jay's grandparents came from Delhi, in India, but he was born in Britain. Indian culture existed for thousands of years, long before British people went there. They treated Indians as if British culture was better than Indian culture. But Jay is proud of both his Indian and British cultures.

Is Ade an African name?

"Yes, it is. It is a Nigerian word meaning "royal." One day, I'd like to visit Jamaica where my parents first lived. My great-great-grandparents were born in Africa. Europeans took them across the sea to Jamaica and made them work there as slaves. But all over the world, people from different cultures won the fight to end slavery."

Racism Today

Katie and Jamila are looking at a globe. Jamila is showing Katie how she traveled from her country, Sudan, to the United States. Jamila is a refugee. Refugees are people who are forced to leave their countries because of war or disaster. Many wars are caused by racists stirring up hatred between people.

We can't stay here, it's not safe.

Why did your parents leave your country?

Because of a war caused by racists.

Story: Repeating Remarks

1 Mike's big sister, Jane, did not like the Indian family across the street.

2 Jane was prejudiced about Indian people. She complained about them to Mike.

3 Later Mike repeated Jane's racist remarks to Ranjit. Ranjit was upset.

Why did Mike hurt Ranjit?

Mike repeated what Jane had said, without thinking. If he had thought about it, he would not have said unfair things. For Ranjit and the Indian family opposite, home is here. They have every right to be here. Racist ideas are learned from others. If friends or members of your family are racist, try to think for yourself. Tell them what you think.

▲ Green Or Yellow?

Racism divides people into groups based on culture or skin color. Dividing people in this way is as silly as saying you can only play with others wearing the same color shirt as you. But we all belong to one race—the HUMAN RACE!

◀ Racism Is Always Wrong

Anyone can be racist, whatever his or her skin color, religion, or culture. Sometimes people blame those from other cultures for problems in the world. This is unfair and not true. There is never any excuse for racism.

Katie, have you ever been in a gang?

"I was in Jake's gang. It was great at first but then some people in the gang started being mean about Jamila and my African friends. I didn't want to be mean to Jamila, but I was scared to tell Jake he was wrong. In the end, I told Jake what I thought of him. I left his gang. I'm really glad I did, and now Jamila is my good friend."

▶ Unfair Treatment

A person may be stopped from getting a job or a place at school because of his or her skin color or culture. This is racism. It is against the law, but it can take a long time to change people's ideas.

▲ Gangs

It can be fun to be in a gang. But it is not fun if there are racist bullies in a gang. Racist gangs attack people from different cultures or pick fights with other gangs.

▶ Hope For The Future

Things can change however. In South Africa, white people tried to rule black people using racist laws, under a system called apartheid. This system ended in 1990. Since then, former President Nelson Mandela and other politicians in South Africa have tried to make sure that everybody is treated fairly.

Feelings

Aaron and Phoebe are talking about how it feels when someone is racist. Aaron said when Jake picked on him, he lay awake at night, and had nightmares when he did fall asleep. Phoebe had to leave her country quickly because of the war there, caused by racists. When she first came here she felt lonely and sad.

Racism can make you worry.

How did racism make you feel?

When people ignored me, I was upset and mad.

Story: Speaking Up

1 Paul and Ken were whispering. Tess heard them say racist things about Craig.

2 Later Tess told her mom what had happened at school. Tess was upset.

3 Tess didn't like what Paul had said, but felt too scared to speak up for Craig.

Why did Tess feel unsure?

Tess felt unhappy about the way Ken and Paul had acted, but felt too scared to say anything. It takes courage to speak out about something you feel is wrong. If you notice someone being racist, try not to ignore it. Think how you feel when someone is rude to you and everyone else ignores the situation.

Feelings

▶ Feeling Low

Racist jokes and comments are very upsetting. They can make you feel miserable and lonely. You might feel sick or find it hard to eat properly. If racism happens at school, it might make you want to stay home from school.

◀ Keep Calm

Racism may make you feel angry. You might want to be racist too, or start a fight. It's OK to feel angry, but fighting back is not the answer. It can get you into trouble and doesn't stop the racism. It is better to tell a grown-up you trust.

▶ It's Not Your Fault

If someone is racist to you, it can make you feel unhappy. It might be hard to concentrate at school. But remember, it is not your fault if someone is being racist. There is nothing wrong with you— it's the racist who is wrong.

▶ Big Or Small

Racism can make you feel sad and unsure of yourself. But try to remember all the things about yourself that you really like. Feeling good about yourself will help you to deal with racist remarks.

◀ Talking It Over

If someone has been racist, it will help to talk about it to someone you trust. Keeping your feelings to yourself won't help. Try talking to your best friend, your mom, dad, carer, or a teacher.

▶ Feeling At Home

When children arrive in a new country, everything is very strange. It can take a while before they learn the new language. People in their school may ignore them. This is unfair and makes them feel scared or angry—they haven't done anything wrong. If there are any new pupils from other countries in your class, try to make them feel at home. Perhaps they would like to be in your team.

Yasmin, how did racism affect you?

"A few girls at school called me names after the terrorist attacks on New York. My mom and dad thought about sending me to a Muslim school but I had lots of friends and didn't want to leave. So they went to see my principal with some of the other parents. There was a class discussion and we talked about my religion, Islam. It was good to explain what being a Muslim is really about. I think it helped other pupils to understand."

Stopping Racism

Tony, Gary, and Connie are talking about how to deal with racism. Connie says you could try ignoring people who are being racist. They might give up if they don't manage to upset you. Tony says he and Gary stood up to Jake when he was being racist and that worked. But sometimes the best thing to do is to tell a grown-up.

Say "No!" to racism.

Story: Hitting Back

1 Meera told her teacher that she was being bullied.

2 Mrs. Bird knew where the gang played. She caught them bullying Meera.

3 Mrs. Bird talked to the gang. They realized that they had been unkind.

Was Meera right to tell?

Yes. Sometimes you will need help to deal with racism. Tell a grown-up you trust. He or she may be able to sort things out, without anyone knowing you have told. If the first person you tell can't help, tell someone else. People who are being racist need to understand that their actions hurt other people. They need to be stopped.

Story: Lee Helps Out

1 Karl was German. Tim and Dave always teased him. This time Lee was there.

2 Lee stood up for Karl. He told Dave and Tim to leave Karl alone.

3 Karl was pleased that Lee had stood up for him.

Was Lee right to help Karl?

Yes. If you see someone being racist, try to help. Doing nothing is not the answer—it will look as if you agree with what the racists say. If people think they can get away with being racist, they will carry on. If you are not sure how to deal with the problem on your own, ask a grown-up who will be able to help sort things out.

▶ Racism Is Bad For Everyone!

Racists miss out on lots of fun and friends, just because they decide about people without getting to know them. If you take the trouble, you may find that you have lots in common with someone from a different culture.

◀ Enjoy Life!

Instead of being scared of differences, you can share and enjoy them! Every little effort that you make to stop racism will make a difference.

Connie, what can be done about racism?

"My class discussed racism. Some people were surprised to find out how upsetting it can be. We all agreed not to let racism happen in our school. We said we would try to help if we saw anyone being racist. Now, when a new girl or boy arrives in our class we look after them and make them feel welcome."

Don't Forget...

1

How can you deal with racism, Ade?

"It's not easy, but there are things you can do. Try to keep calm. Think carefully about the situation. Sometimes, it's better to walk away. At other times it's best to tell a grown-up. Sometimes, you might be able to tell the racist to leave you alone. Try practicing what you're going to say first."

2

What do you think about racism, Yasmin?

"Racists miss out on lots of friendships, just because of their silly ideas about people. We know it's hard, but try not to let racists make you feel unhappy. Tell your good friends how you feel. Good friends help you feel good."

How does your school deal with racism, Jon?

"Our school is very strict about racism. We all agreed that our school should be a safe place for everyone. We don't allow racism to happen because it affects everyone, whatever his or her culture. We all have a right to feel happy."

3

4

Is it right to tell a grown-up about racism, Katie?

"It's not tattling to talk to a grown-up about racism. It's often the best thing to do, especially if you feel unsure about dealing with a difficult situation by yourself. Tell a teacher, a playground helper, your mom, dad, or carer. Racism is wrong. It's important that we all try to stop racism."

Find Out More About Racism

Helpful Addresses and Phone Numbers

Talking about problems can really help. If you can't talk to someone close to you, then try phoning one of these organizations:

Just For Kids Hotline
Tel: 1-888-594-kids
A 24-hour free helpline for children. The number won't show up on a telephone bill.

National Youth Crisis Hotline
Tel: 800-442-HOPE (442-4673)
Provides services for children and youth who are depressed over family or school problems.
Operates 24 hours.

Kids Help Phone, Canada
Tel: 1-800-668-6868
Toll-free anywhere in Canada.
English or French, 24 hours a day, 365 days a year.

Amnesty International
Tel: (613) 744-7667
1-800-AMNESTY (266-3789)
info@amnesty.ca
www.amnesty.ca
Deals with issues of justice, equality, and freedom.

Child Welfare League of America
Tel: (202) 638 2952
www.cwla.org
A confidential helpline offering advice for parents and children.

On the Web

These websites are also helpful. You can get in touch with some of them using email:

www.childhelpusa.org

www.kidshelpphone.ca/en

www.youthinformation.com

www.all4all.org

www.bullyonline.org

www.servingourworld.org

www.magenta.nl/crosspoint/us.html

Further Reading

If you want to read more about racism, try:

Talking About: Racism
by Bruce Sanders (Stargazer Books)

Choices and Decisions: Dealing with Racism by Pete Sanders and Steve Myers (Stargazer Books)

What's That Got to Do With Me?: Racism by Antony Lishak (Franklin Watts)

Everyday Racism
by Annie S. Barnes (Barnes)

What Do We Think About: Racism
by Jen Green (Hodder Wayland)

Get Wise: Racism and Prejudice
by Jane Bingham (Heinemann)

Index

Photocredits

l-left, r-right, b-bottom, t-top, c-center, m-middle

All photos from istockphoto.com except: Cover tl , 24, 27—DAJ.

11, 13, 16—Brand X Pictures. 14 , 17—Select Pictures/Marc Arundale.

All the photos in this book have been posed by models.